Field Manual for Effective Leadership

By Steve S. Aslan

PAGE PUBLISHING, INC.
New York, NY

First originally published by Page Publishing, Inc. 2014

ISBN 978-1-62838-466-6 (pbk)
ISBN 978-1-62838-467-3 (digital)

Printed in the United States of America

Topics

- Effective Leaders
- Direction and Clarity
- Prioritizing
- Consistency
- Respect
- Communicating
- Goal Setting
- Teams
- Coaching and Counseling
- Investigations
- Summary

Effective Leaders And Their Traits

Clarity

Direction

Prioritize

BUILD TEAMS

Consistent

Set Goals

Respect

Effective Leaders

Communicate clearly

- When they are done speaking or writing you understand what they said
- They allow and request questions. Why?
- Clarity includes writing and speaking with words that are **simple, precise, descriptive** and **at the level of the audience**
- **Tone** is extremely important. Why?

- Forum or location of your message

- Awareness of the speed you are transmitting

- Match your message with the correct target members or you will lose your audience and effectiveness

- Be visual, provide examples, show relationships

- Tell them what you are going to tell them, then at the end, summarize what you have just told them

Direction

- Why is direction important to a leader and what does that mean?

- Direction defines for us the place where we want to end up

- Direction is critical in determining how long it will take to get where we want to go

- Forces us to evaluate what resources we may need

- Good direction is not only about defining the path/direction but visibility of what surrounds the path (goal, objective, or task)

- If you and your team don't know your direction, failed results are certain to abound

- The directions must be clear and understood by all

- Review previous topic, **Clarity,** to ensure a leader's effectiveness

If a man does not know what forest he is in, no map will be enough to guide him
(Direction and Clarity)

Prioritizing

Why is it important?
How do you do it?

- It is important because it:
  - Forces you to identify the most important tasks to attack first
  - Ensures you have evaluated the amount of **time** it will take to accomplish the tasks. Knowing this allows you to slot/prioritize what gets done and when
  - Requires you to do **planning**

- Identifies value:
  - Time to achieve vs. reward or metric it results in
  - Focuses and defines what **needs** to be done vs. what you want to do
  - Keeps you organized
  - Saves time and money
  - Identifies where most project value and profitability is
  - It is your time manager tool
  - Aligns what the company priority is with what yours should be
  - **Objective**: Organize so that tasks, objectives, and goals can be ranked and ordered ensuring the most urgent and important ones are accomplished first, second, third, etc..
  - Measure the **time and resources** available and compare with the level of value that will result
  - Understand the difference between **urgent** and **important**
  - Determine what will deliver the biggest value
  - If necessary, get clarification from your boss

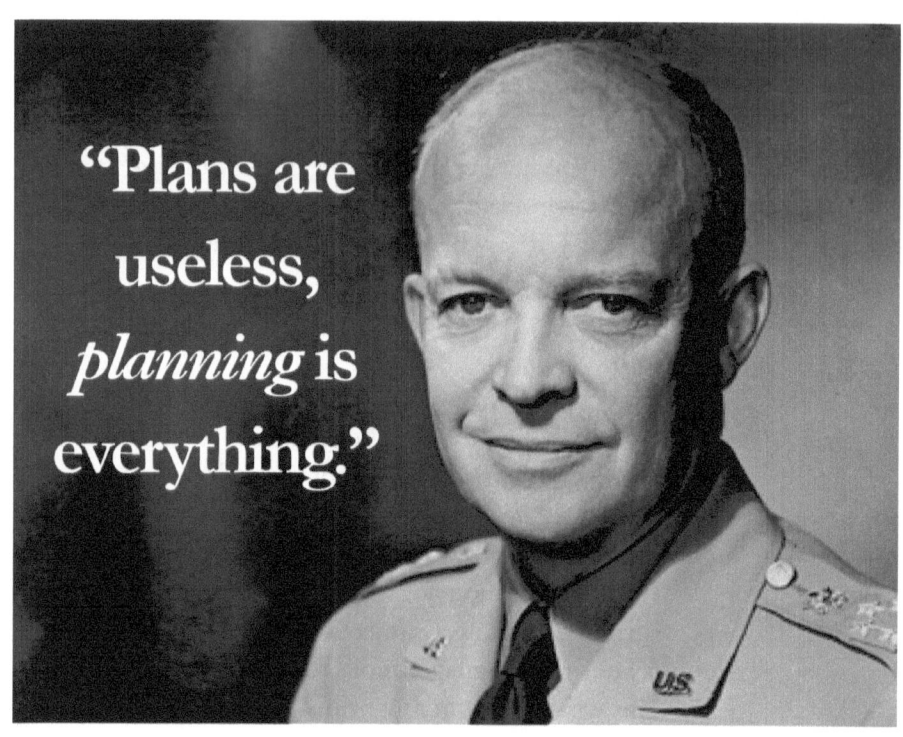

Quoting General Dwight Eisenhower

Methods of Prioritizing

Various Methods:

ABCDE Method:

- Apply letters in the margin and list the tasks to each
    - A = Very Important
    - B = Important
    - C = Should do (less important than A,B)
    - D = Delegate
    - E = Eliminate

- When in doubt of level of importance, check with your boss

Methods of Prioritizing
Urgent vs. Important

Important, Not Urgent **This is your next priority and should be completed second** • **Importance has high priority status** **Do second**	*Important and Urgent* **This is your top priority and should be completed first** • **Importance generally trumps urgent** **Do first**
Not Important, But Urgent This priority should be evaluated with your boss and should be measured for when they can be slipped in and immediately completed • Identify for immediate opportunity to complete following Important, Not Urgent **Complete in coordination with bosses evaluation of need**	*Not Important and Not Urgent* This priority should be evaluated for elimination or reprioritization amongst remaining objectives • Review list for reorganization **Delegate or eliminate**

Consistency

- What is consistency and why is it important?

- Pronounced: con·sist·en·cy

- A noun

- Conformity in the application of something, typically that which is necessary for the sake of logic, accuracy, or fairness

- Synonyms: uniformity, constancy, regularity, evenness, steadiness, stability, equilibrium, reliability, predictability

- It's important at work and in business because it:
  - **Reduces the stress** of communication by the boss and among the team, by knowing what kind and type of response can be expected
  - **Entices repeat business** and interactions by whoever you support, serve, or have a relationship with, provided it is positive (think of **McDonald's**—it is consistent everywhere in the world). The reverse is true when consistency is not delivered
  - **Builds trust.** Consistent behavior builds trust because your people and your team know what to expect and how you will support and react to them

- Is important because:
  - It makes things (processes, behaviors, relationships, communication) **flow in sync** and smoothly, with evenness, reliability, and predictability
    - Aids in knowing what the outcome will be or is expected to be
  - It will either support or inhibit your team from coming to you for leadership or much of anything else

- Can you think of why this is true?
  - Inconsistent behavior may result in fear from your subordinates when you display huge swings in responses and reactions. This will likely result in your team-members failure to seek you out

Be Consistent

- To be consistent, you must be:
  - **In control**—ability to react the same each time despite how things change (e.g. restraint, adjust for situation, check your attitude)
  - **Awareness of self**—regulate and adjust
  - **Act**, don't react
    - Pause
    - Take a breath
    - Listen entirely, think and think logically, respond with evenness
    - Focus on your tone, body language, choice of words, energy level

- To be consistent, you must be:
  - Aware of how you are going to respond before you actually take action
  - Reacting and responding with the same logic, reasoning, and communication style each and every time
  - Focused on a **response** that is given **without fear** of being challenged
    - Open
    - Receptive
    - Factual
    - Understanding of the issue
    - Determined to fix the issue (forget the blame)
    - Nonconfrontational and Nondefensive
    - Prepared to keep your promises
    - Accountable and honest for your every action
  - Practice, practice, practice (at home, in the store, on the phone, writing, etc.)

Consistency

*"It's not what we do once in a while that shapes our lives.
It's what we do consistently."*
-Anthony Robbins

And it applies to Leadership. In other words, it's not what we do once in a while that shapes our **leadership effectiveness**. It's what we do consistently.

Respect

- Has various definitions, and our focuses are:
  - A feeling or understanding that someone or something is important, serious, etc., and should be treated in an appropriate way
  - A feeling of admiring someone or something that is good, valuable, important, etc.
  - A particular way of thinking about or looking at something
  - A polite greeting or expression of kind feelings
  - As a polite or formal way of saying that you disagree with someone

- Is important because it:
  - Makes us human having morals and ethics
  - Shows understanding and awareness that other people are important, have value, and are deserving of the same treatment you would like to have
  - Affirms reasonableness, allowing for open communication and sharing of information

- What good is it?
  - Gives you a humanness that brings people to you

- "The day soldiers stop bringing you their problems is the day you have stopped leading them. They have either lost confidence that you can help them or concluded that you do not care. Either case is a failure of leadership."–Colin Powell

- It is required to build a team!
- It affects your performance, the team, and the company
- **It is the root in creating:**
  - Open communication —confidence to speak up
  - Begins the process of building trust
  - Allows for maximum productivity
  - Engaged and contributing employees
  - The most successful environment
  - A work environment employees want to be a part of and stay with

Respect

On the Flip Side

What happens when respect is **not shown** to people you engage with?

- Big productivity loss

- They distrust you

- Become disengaged

- They talk

- You lose their creativity

- Visibility you don't want

- They shut down

- Potential law suits

Respect

Can I Get Some?

- If you give it, you will receive it. It must be earned
    - Send a feeling that you care—empathize
    - Listen with interest
        - It shows you value their opinion
    - Understand that you/they may think differently
    - Be open to receiving their ideas
    - Be calm and nonconfrontational
    - Always respond and follow up

RESPECT

"Never hold discussions with the monkey when the organ grinder is in the room."

W. Churchill speaking with Franklin D. Roosevelt

Communication

- An act or instance of transmitting or conveying information

- A process by which information is exchanged between individuals through a common system of symbols, signs, or behavior; verbal or written message

- A two-way process that involves a sender and receiver

Communication Feedback Loop

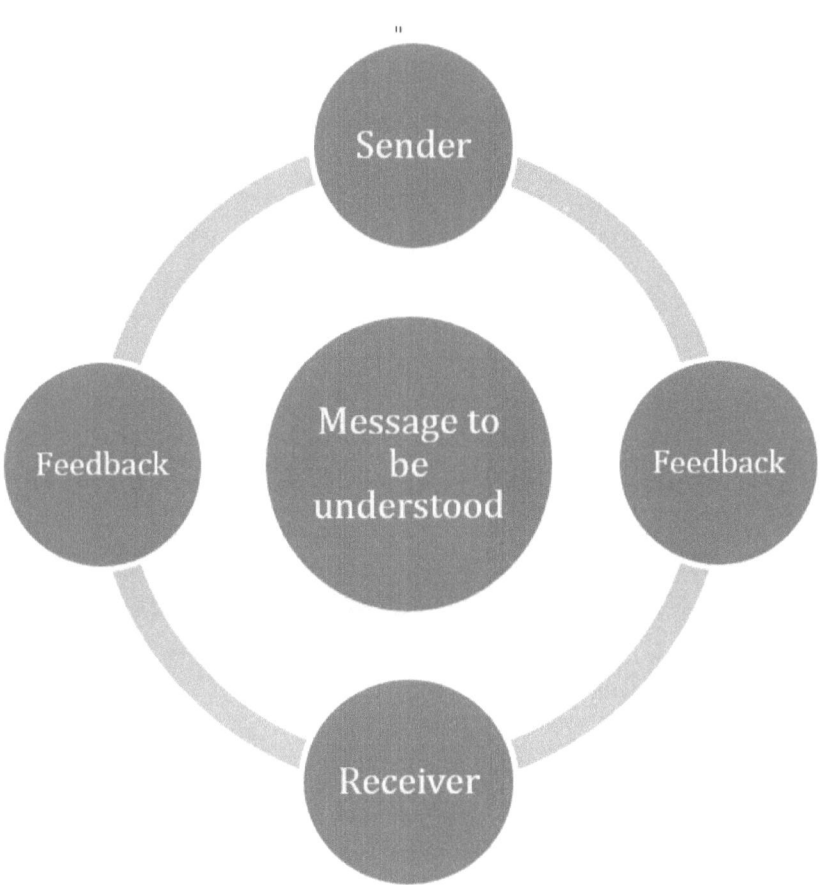

Good Communication Results

There are good communication results when:

- The sender and receiver are honest and forthright

- Questions and clarifications are requested and delivered

- Feedback is exchanged

- Both sender and receiver transmit and relay back to each other that they understand the message

- Appropriate words and descriptions are used to convey your point

- You look each other in the eyes comfortably

- You moderate your tone and body language to suit the audience
  - Small audience, less body language; large audience, more pronounced use of body language

- Both sender and receiver are open to what is or might be said for the **purpose of understanding**

- Both or all parties listen and listen completely, without interruption

- Respect and trust for solutions, rather than power, power plays, and confrontation drive the discussion

- Both are clear, crisp, concise, and complete

- You engage / come to the discussion bias free and attitude neutral

- Practice, practice, practice

When Communication Is Poor

The man asked for help on how to launch his boat. He was told to "put the trailer in the water until the back wheels reach the water."

Goal Setting

Alice in Wonderland

Cat: Where are you going?
Alice: Which way should I go?
Cat: That depends on where you are going.
Alice: I don't know.
Cat: Then it doesn't matter which way you go.
— Lewis Carroll, *Alice in Wonderland*

Write it down. Written goals have a way of transforming wishes into wants; cant's into cans; dreams into plans; and plans into reality.

Don't just think it – ink it! —Author Unknown

Goal Setting

How To

S.M.A.R.T. Goals
- S - Specific
- M - Measurable
- A - Achievable
- R - Relevant
- T - Time Bound

- **Specific**
  - Ensures the goal is detailed by including who, what, where, when, why, and how—but it is not necessary to use all of them
  - Use verbs and adverbs for defining it
  - Produce, deliver, implement, design, etc.
  - Provides clarity
  - It should define what needs to be accomplished by when

- **Measurable**
  - A method to gauge the value of a goal which is either numeric or descriptive
  - It can describe a quantity, a cost, quality, timeliness, effectiveness, completeness, flexibility, etc.
  - Describes the level of success or achievement
  - It identifies the value of the outcome and not the actions of the task, objectives, or goal

- Achievable

The goal is reasonable and the outcome is obtainable given consideration of following:
  - Resources are available?
    - Individuals/Team
    - Money
    - Tools and Equipment
  - Time available
  - Level of Knowledge, Skills and Abilities (KSA's) are within the individual or team
  - Authority or Sphere of Control (SoC)
    - Influence, impact and affect across other departments and processes

- Relevant

  - The goals should be applicable to the department and a cascade from the top meeting the organization's mission, vision, goals, objectives, and tasks
  - Ask yourself:
    - Does this goal align with the department's goals
    - Why is this goal important
    - How much value will this goal bring to the department and organization
    - Does it align with our key success factors (KSF)

- Time Bound:
  - The goal should identify times, dates, timetables (for partial or subparts) specifying when the goals or objectives are to be achieved and completed
  - Allow for organization – *"The only reason for time is so that everything doesn't happen at once."*—**Albert Einstein**
  - Inspires action
  - Eliminate or reduce desperation by creating order, structure, and sequencing
  - Allows **others** to plan their work priorities
  - Provides a visual and mental reminder
  - Aids in taking follow-up action
  - Tool for tracking progress
  - Ultimately puts clarity and understanding between the supervisor and employee on the timeliness and deadline for completion of the goal

Goal Setting

SMART Method

Practice Examples

Non-SMART Goal: Maintain and keep the company website up-to-date.

SMART Goal: By the end of business each day, I will have made all changes to and updates to the website along with written documentation of each change made and the date it was completed.

Non-SMART Goal: Apply this leadership course to each employee I engage.

SMART Goal: I will find 10 colleagues or friends over the next 90 days and practice using the chapters on Communication, Direction and Respect by implementing what I have learned. I will request feedback from them and write a summary of what I learned.

Non-SMART Goal: Sell 95 percent of widgets to our customers by the end of the year.

SMART Goal: I will sell 125 frames and 75 mats each month to Acme, Law Metals, Firm Supply, and RX Company. And I will sell at least 10 bundles of 5 sets to our top 5 customers by the end of the second quarter.

Modeling Teams

- Discipline

- Coaching

- Team Building
  - How to build them
  - How to train them
  - How to motivate them
  - How to develop them
  - How to retain them
  - How they teach others to learn how to lead

Teams
(How to Build Them)

- How to build them
  - A leader must be selected and recognized
  - The leader must:
    - Have an absolute understanding of what is needed to accomplish the objectives for success
    - Determine the number of team members needed
    - Determine the level of experiences, skills, knowledge and abilities (KSA), and expertise required by each member
    - Match the members to the task and to each and every other member That includes the following:
      - Gain respect of **all** members or you will have a weak link (which might create contagious negativity)
      - Be able to motivate and keep the members engaged
      - Set the examples and hold him/herself to a higher standard
      - Prove his value, expertise, and intelligence

- For successful teams they need to:
  - Have **all** members communicating extremely well with every member of the team
    - No holding back, open, sharing, supporting (each has each other's back), no politics or hidden agendas
  - Have 100 percent focus on the mission, objectives, or tasks at hand (it must be viewed as bigger than they are)
  - Commitment and cooperation
  - Creativity: out-of-the-box thinking to solve problems
  - Connections and networks for support
  - Be flexible
    - Ready, open, and able to **adapt and accept and execute**
  - Contribute
    - To each other and to the objectives overall
  - Confidence
    - In themselves and their team members
  - Driven to succeed regardless of difficulties and challenges

- Training
  - For maximum effectiveness, every team member must be an expert at what they do
  - Skills that are missing must be acquired and without delay
  - Training must be practiced and updated
  - A theory or process is useless if you can't put it into practice or place so it can be executed

- Help your teams learn
  - Tell them why training is important
  - What they are expected to know when they exit
  - Use as many senses as possible to reinforce the training
    - Visual, auditory, touch
    - Demonstrate it
  - Use it, do something with it, experiment
  - Test them
  - Practice and repeat

Teams
How to Train Them

- Provide experts to deliver the training

- Make sure your team members have the ability and aptitude to learn the training
  - Pick the right members for the job

- Ensure prerequisites are met
  - Think vertical
    - bottom up (for complete understanding)

- Give them the tools and resources necessary to become experts

- Invest the time and money or don't expect maximized performance or success

Team Training is Vital

"The only easy day was yesterday" —Navy Seals

Teams
How to Motivate Them

- Motivating your team requires:
  - An understanding of why they are here
  - Defining what value they provide
  - Knowing this is something bigger than they as individuals are
  - Receiving recognition for a job well done
  - Show them you are:
    - Bright, in control, driven, hands-on and always "have their backs" (especially in public), and successful

- Developing your team requires:
  - Interactive and ongoing conversations and communication of where they want to be in the future
  - Feedback: if you don't know where you are, you will never get to where you want to be
  - A written and time-driven accountable plan of the things you need to learn and accomplish
  - Providing the tools, resources, and training to meet the developmental plan in place
  - Giving the opportunity to succeed
    - Put in the position to show what you learned or will learn (lead)
  - Concluding and completing the cycle with feedback
  - Continuously improving on what you learned
    - Apply those learned KSAs to your next set of development objectives

Teams
How to Retain Them

- Huge investment—now what?

- You have:
  - Selected them
  - Trained them
  - Motivated them
  - Developed them

- Make sure you keep them!

- Retaining your team:
  - **You must continue to lead them**

- Be visible and engage them daily
  - Ask them for input and feedback
  - Let them help you solve the challenges
    - Give them responsibility, accountability, authority and get out of their way

- Provide constant performance feedback

- Discuss their next career movements and desires

- Recognize them publicly and privately

- Reward them

- **Keep them challenged:**
  - Give them new projects (best if they champion it)
  - Let them travel
  - Put them on cross-functional teams
  - Send them off-site for training / instruction / conferences / just for information or networking

- **Just tell them thank you!**

Remember Colin Powell's quote:

"Leadership is solving problems. The day soldiers stop bringing you their problems is the day you have stopped leading them. They have either lost confidence that you can help or concluded you do not care. Either case is a failure of leadership."

Teams
Leading

- At this point in the field, you and/or your team members are leaders!
  - You have learned besides being taught
    - Experience and execution makes a leader

- A leader's most important responsibility and requirement is to:
  - **"Give Other's An Opportunity To Lead"**
    - Share and show, set the example
    - Give power away
    - **Let them be the example**

- Put them in positions to lead!
  - And they will rise to succeed

- Get out of the way

- Trust

Performance Management Coach, Counsel, Investigate, and Discipline

- Once your team is assembled, you will need to monitor and communicate their performance

- You will need to review the chapters on motivation and retention

- And at some time, you will have to coach, counsel, investigate, and discipline

Coaching and Counseling

- Coaching
  - When you want good behaviors to continue
    - Re-enforces change in a POSITIVE way
    - More informal

- Counseling
  - When you want poor behaviors to change
    - Identified as a need to change NEGATIVE behavior
    - More formal
  - Timely (usually close to when it occurs)
  - Provides effective feedback
  - Specific, detailed
  - Privately delivered
  - Face-to-face
  - Honest , direct, and open

Coaching and Counseling Key Points

- Delivered in a calm, professional, even-toned voice

- Supervisor must stay in control of the delivery

- Provide the employee with opportunity to give feedback

- Should not be confrontational but end in understanding

- Decide: Is this a coaching issue or a counseling issue? Handle accordingly

- Coaching
  - Behavior you want to continue
  - Behavior is not dangerous or severe but needs to be brought to one's attention
  - Small issues
  - First or second time it has ever happened

Coaching

- Reinforcing the positive

- Generally it's the best approach
  - Conduct the meeting in private
    - Use ice breaker or safe introduction
      Hi Sam, how are things going? I just wanted to thank you for x and lend some thoughts about yesterday's meeting.
  - Point out positives first, with specifics
  - Follow up with your observations with key specifics you would like to see enhanced or changed

- You can say, *"Sam, I wanted to let you know when you do x, it results in y to others watching you. I think if you work on z, it will greatly improve and enhance your image, presentation, etc."*
  - This approach is a good way to introduce "coaching" change your desire to the team member. It is honest, direct feedback with tact, suggesting how you may improve
  - Provide specific feedback where a slight change would enhance the current behavior/actions
  - Be a coach!
    - Picture how you would like someone to help you out and do the same for them

Counseling:
Key Points

- Counseling
  - Unsatisfactory performance
  - Failure to meet job requirements
  - Poor behavior (excessive absenteeism, disrespect, unsatisfactory working, insubordination, relationships, safety and PPE violations)
  - Failure of supervisor or manager to develop, direct or lead a team

Investigations

- Once your team is assembled, you will need to manage their performance

- You will need to review the chapter Coaching and Counseling

- You will at some point have to conduct investigations. At some point, you will have to conduct an investigation into an employee's allegation that they were wronged by someone in some way

- You must conduct an investigation at that point when you are informed or observed actions or behaviors violating policy, procedures, standards, ethics or criminal issues

- Interview the complainant first

- Create an "I want to assist you" relationship

- Keep a totally open and impartial objective view

- Tell them you need them to be extremely specific
  - If they are not, you must ask for the details and specifics before they leave the room
- Take every detail of notes
  - Date them, read them back to the employee, and have them give you their agreement that this is the entire story and your notes are correct. Have them sign and date the notes
- Assure them that only the people with a need to know will the notes be shared with
- Assure them, if anyone tries to retaliate, that they will be severely disciplined up to and including termination
- Gathering the facts:
  - Are there witnesses?
    - Be sure and interview every one of them
  - Are there notes or a log of previous incidences that the complainant has documented or recorded?
- Gathering the facts:
  - Has the employee discussed this with anyone else?
  - Put the facts in chronological order with dates, times, places, witnesses
- Determine if this is a pattern or isolated
- Ask the employee what outcome would you like to see or have happen

- Interview the subject of the complaint:
  - Again, start with building a safe environment for communication
  - State what the issue is and why you are speaking with them. Be forthright and impartial
    - You want to hear their side of the story with all the same open and impartialness as possible
    - **Later** in the conversation, you can become more critical, specific, and focused on getting the truth, the whole truth

- Interviewing the subject of the complaint

- Get the details:
  - Ask the tough, embarrassing, "white elephant in the room" questions
  - Identify the areas of violations to policy, ethics, procedures, criminal points of the complaint
  - Point out the seriousness and consequences of falsifying information or details
    - Ensure they understand the importance and consequences of this investigation

- Interviewing the subject of the complaint

- Be sure to put things in chronological order and point out the gaps

- If you feel they are lying, withholding information, or state the complainant is lying, ask them why someone would do that

- Ask for all documents, records, and proof that they have

- Be sure to compare what they say to the complainant's story and point out where it does not match up or is a gap
  - ASK THE TOUGH QUESTIONS.
- Have them read the notes and sign and date them
- Review all notes and make notes and questions for follow-up
  - Make notes about each person's behavior(nervousness, tone, words, posture)
- Get answers to gaps or other necessary pieces to get the full picture
- Make a summary of findings (it helps organize your facts)
- Make a recommendation based on just the FACTS
- Use the facts to validate that there was or was not a violation of policy, practice, ethics, criminal, or other wronged behavior
- You may want to bring both parties together when having a final resolution
  - Be aware that it may be a very confrontational situation or it may bring both parties to an understanding
- Have another person review your conclusion and recommendation

- Do not terminate in haste
  - Be sure you have all your facts and findings solid
  - Are you willing to go to court over this? This question is a good gauge on your decision

- Ask the complainant if they are satisfied or if there is another option or recommendation they seek to help resolve this

- Assure all parties that this will be kept completely confidential

Investigation Follow-up

- Once the investigation is completed, you must decide if further action is to be taken

- Generally, there is always some kind of documentation to summarize the findings, which must delineate a final response

- At this point, some kind of discipline is given to adjust for improper behavior

- This discipline is called **progressive discipline**

Progressive Discipline

- General order with increasing severity
  - However, we can sidestep the progression should we decide we need to

- Generally, this is the order:
  - Verbal (supervisor makes notes for self)
  - Written (1–2 letters to file)
  - Performance improvement plan (PIP)
  - Suspension (unpaid)
  - Termination

Summary

Leadership Effectiveness

- Effective leadership comes from many actions taken by an individual
  - Physical, mental, oral, written, and visible

- Other characteristics not covered can enhance a leader's effectiveness, but today's topics will absolutely build and advance your leadership effectiveness

- Focus on the Following:
  - Direction and clarity
  - Prioritizing
  - Consistency
  - Respect
  - Communicating
  - Goal setting

- As with most behaviors and actions, excellence, effectiveness, and success comes to those who practice, practice, practice

*"Before you are a leader, success is all about growing yourself.
When you become a leader, success is all about growing others."*

—Jack Welch

Steve Aslan Quote

If you provide **direction** *with* **clarity** *through* **goals** *and then*
prioritize *how you will get there while being* **consistent**,
you will earn the **respect** *of your* **team**
and that will make you a better **leader**.

GonetotheSnowDogs.com

Effective leaders can take any shape or be in any position.

About the Author

Steve S. Aslan resides in upstate New York with his wife, Carla, and two daughters, Amanda and Lauren.

Over the past twenty years Steve has worked in the field of Human Resources in various industries. He has a Master's of Science in Human Resources Management and Development from Chapman University, CA and a bachelor degree in Geology. He knows about being a leader after spending more than 9 years as a Naval Officer and learning how to follow and learn how his leaders behaved, acted and executed. For three years, he worked as a Naval Officer in the position of the "Officer in Charge" of the Defense Mapping Agency Operations in the Philippines where he received the Joint Commendation Medal for all his hard work.

Steve's book is about the tools, traits and methods to practice with the purpose of developing, enhancing, and guiding you to become a more effective leader. He noticed, felt and experienced very few leaders in the private world of business that left him with a feeling he would do ANYTHING for them. Steve believed he would grow and succeed by sticking with them, and giving them his unbridled support, up to and including his life for the sake of meeting the mission.

He would like to thank his wife and two daughters, brother, Stacy and sister, Carole, mother, Monique, and father, Ed, for being his biggest support system.